Piano ~ Vocal ~ Guitar

cmt 100 greatest
love songs

W9-ANB-304

ISBN 0-634-08650-2

HAL•LEONARD®
CORPORATION

7777 W. BLUEMOUND RD. P.O. BOX 13819 MILWAUKEE, WI 53213

Visit Hal Leonard Online at
www.halleonard.com

cmt 100 greatest love songs

Rank	Song	Artist	Year
1.	I Will Always Love You	*Dolly Parton*	1974, 1982
2.	Always on My Mind	*Willie Nelson*	1982
3.	Sweet Dreams	*Patsy Cline*	1963
4.	Forever and Ever, Amen	*Randy Travis*	1987
5.	Hello Darlin'	*Conway Twitty*	1970
6.	Unanswered Prayers	*Garth Brooks*	1991
7.	Amazed	*Lonestar*	2000
8.	She Believes in Me	*Kenny Rogers*	1979
9.	I Cross My Heart	*George Strait*	1992
10.	Golden Ring	*George Jones & Tammy Wynette*	1976
11.	That's the Way Love Goes	*Merle Haggard*	1984
12.	When You Say Nothing at All	*Keith Whitley*	1988
13.	He Stopped Loving Her Today	*George Jones*	1980
14.	How Do I Live	*LeAnn Rimes*	1997
15.	It's Your Love	*Tim McGraw*	1997
16.	Stand by Your Man	*Tammy Wynette*	1968
17.	Kiss an Angel Good Mornin'	*Charley Pride*	1971
18.	I Fall to Pieces	*Patsy Cline*	1961
19.	Feels So Right	*Alabama*	1981
20.	Behind Closed Doors	*Charlie Rich*	1973
21.	Breathe	*Faith Hill*	2000
22.	When I Call Your Name	*Vince Gill*	1990
23.	I'm So Lonesome I Could Cry	*Hank Williams*	1949
24.	Ring of Fire	*Johnny Cash*	1963
25.	Today I Started Loving You Again	*Merle Haggard*	1968
26.	I Swear	*John Michael Montgomery*	1994
27.	I Can't Stop Loving You	*Ray Charles*	1962
28.	Gentle on My Mind	*Glen Campbell*	1967
29.	Strawberry Wine	*Deana Carter*	1996
30.	You're Still the One	*Shania Twain*	1998
31.	You Look So Good in Love	*George Strait*	1984
32.	Lady	*Kenny Rogers*	1980
33.	I Can't Help It (If I'm Still in Love with You)	*Hank Williams*	1951
34.	Mama He's Crazy	*The Judds*	1984
35.	Wichita Lineman	*Glen Campbell*	1968
36.	Annie's Song	*John Denver*	1974
37.	The Woman in Me (Needs the Man in You)	*Shania Twain*	1995
38.	Make the World Go Away	*Eddy Arnold*	1965
39.	On the Other Hand	*Randy Travis*	1986
40.	For the Good Times	*Ray Price*	1970
41.	This Kiss	*Faith Hill*	1998
42.	When I Said I Do	*Clint Black*	1999
43.	Angel Flying Too Close to the Ground	*Willie Nelson*	1981
44.	Before the Next Teardrop Falls	*Freddy Fender*	1975
45.	I Still Believe in You	*Vince Gill*	1992
46.	Louisiana Woman, Mississippi Man	*Loretta Lynn/ Conway Twitty*	1973
47.	Love in the First Degree	*Alabama*	1981
48.	Could I Have This Dance	*Anne Murray*	1980
49.	He'll Have to Go	*Jim Reeves*	1959
50.	She Thinks I Still Care	*George Jones*	1962
51.	Please Remember Me	*Tim McGraw*	1999
52.	El Paso	*Marty Robbins*	1959
53.	Help Me Make It Through the Night	*Sammi Smith*	1971

* Omitted from this publication because of licensing restrictions

Contents

ALWAYS LATE WITH YOUR KISSES

Words and Music by BLACKIE CRAWFORD
and LEFTY FRIZZELL

ALWAYS ON MY MIND

Words and Music by WAYNE THOMPSON,
MARK JAMES and JOHNNY CHRISTOPHER

AMANDA

Words and Music by
BOB McDILL

AMAZED

Words and Music by CHRIS LINDSEY,
MARV GREEN and AIMEE MAYO

Moderately slow Country Ballad

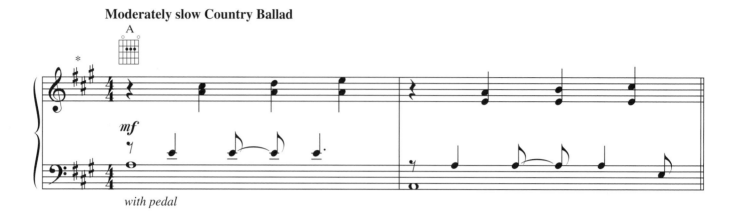

with pedal

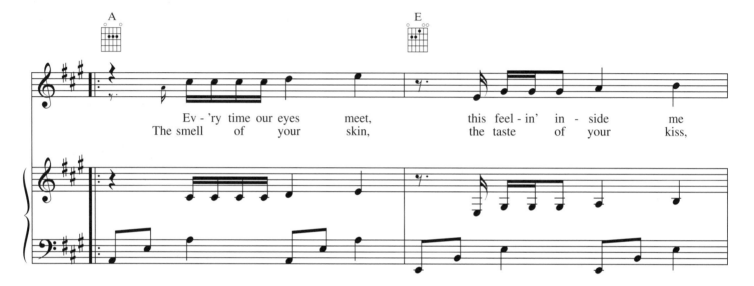

Ev - 'ry time our eyes   meet,   this feel - in' in - side   me
The smell   of   your   skin,   the taste   of   your   kiss,

is al - most more___ than I___ can take.___
the way you whis - per in___ the dark.___

*Recorded a half step lower.

ANGEL OF THE MORNING

Words and Music by
CHIP TAYLOR

Repeat and Fade

ANGEL FLYING TOO CLOSE TO THE GROUND

Words and Music by
WILLIE NELSON

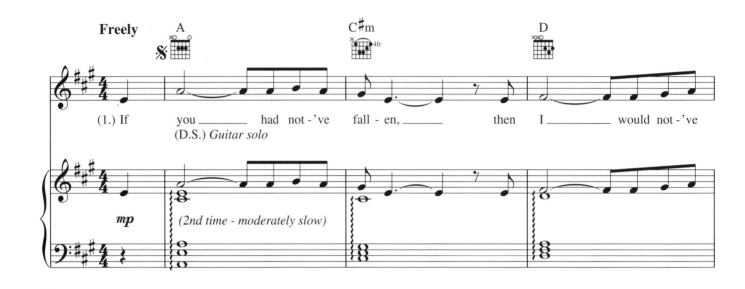

(1.) If you _____ had not-'ve fall-en, _____ then I _____ would not-'ve
(D.S.) *Guitar solo*

mp

(2nd time - moderately slow)

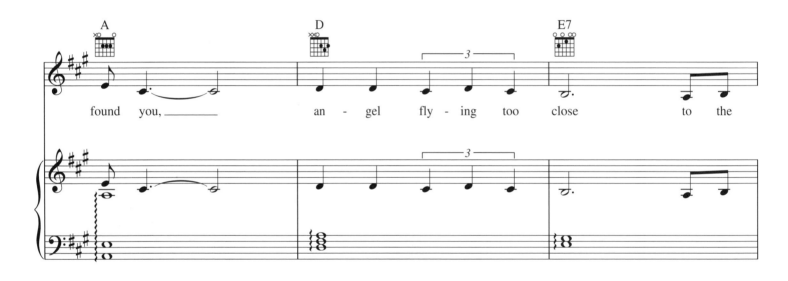

found you, _____ an-gel fly-ing too close to the

Moderately slow

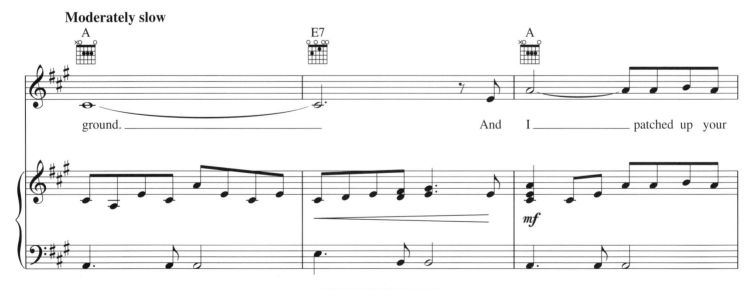

ground. _____ And I _____ patched up your

mf

ANNIE'S SONG

Words and Music by
JOHN DENVER

ANYMORE

Words and Music by TRAVIS TRITT
and JILL COLUCCI

Moderately slow

I can't hide ___ the way ___ I feel ___ a - bout ___
___ one last ___ ap - peal ___ to show ___

___ you how I feel ___ an - y - more. ___
___ you how I feel ___ a - bout you. ___ Mm hm. ___

I could hold ___ the hurt ___ in - side, ___ keep the pain ___
'Cause there's no - one else ___ I swear ___ holds a can -

BEFORE THE NEXT TEARDROP FALLS

Words and Music by BEN PETERS
and VIVIAN KEITH

BEHIND CLOSED DOORS

Words and Music by
KENNY O'DELL

down, and she makes me glad I'm _____ a man; _____ Oh,

no one knows what goes on be-hind closed _____ doors.

My be-hind closed _____ doors. _____

Verse

2. (My) baby makes me smile, Lord, don't she make me smile.
   She's never far away or too tired to say I want you.
   She's always a lady, just like a lady should be
   But when they turn out the lights, she's still a baby to me. **(Chorus)**

COULD I HAVE THIS DANCE

from URBAN COWBOY

Words and Music by WAYLAND HOLYFIELD
and BOB HOUSE

I'll al - ways re - mem - ber the song they were
al - ways re - mem - ber that mag - ic

play - ing the first time _____ we danced and I knew.
mo - ment, when I held _____ you close to me.

As we swayed to the mu - sic _____ and held to each
As we moved to - geth - er, _____ I knew for -

BREATHE

Words and Music by HOLLY LAMAR
and STEPHANIE BENTLEY

Moderately fast

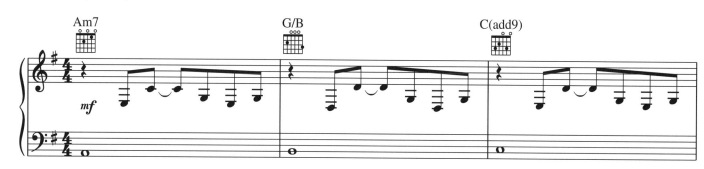

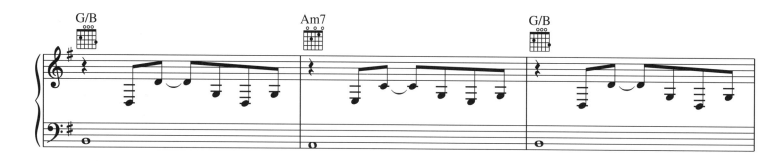

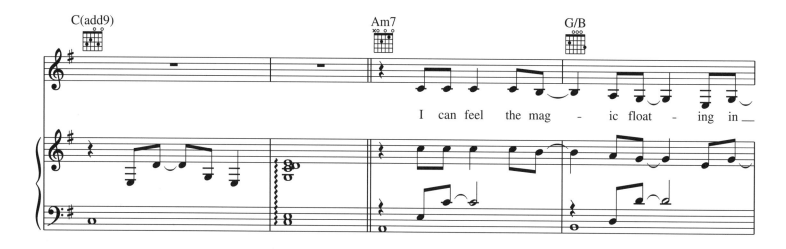

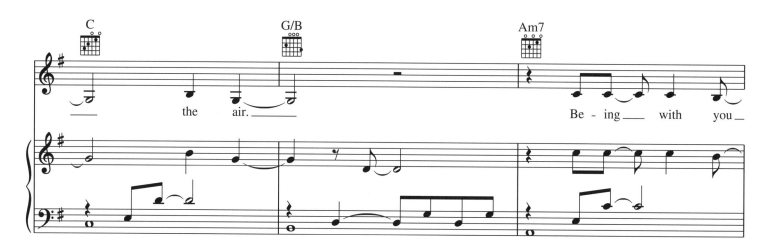

COWBOY TAKE ME AWAY

Words and Music by MARCUS HUMMON
and MARTIE SEIDEL

*Recorded a half step lower.

CRYING

Words and Music by ROY ORBISON
and JOE MELSON

Moderately slow, with feeling

I was all right for a - while;
I was o - ver you but it's

smile for a - while,
true, so true,
but I saw you last night; you held my
I love you e - ven more than I

hand so tight, as you stopped to say, "Hel - lo."
did be - fore, but dar - ling, what can I do?
Oh, you
For you

60

DON'T IT MAKE MY BROWN EYES BLUE

Words and Music by
RICHARD LEIGH

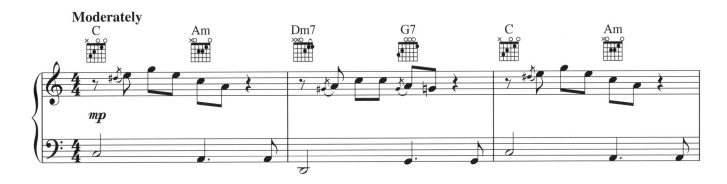

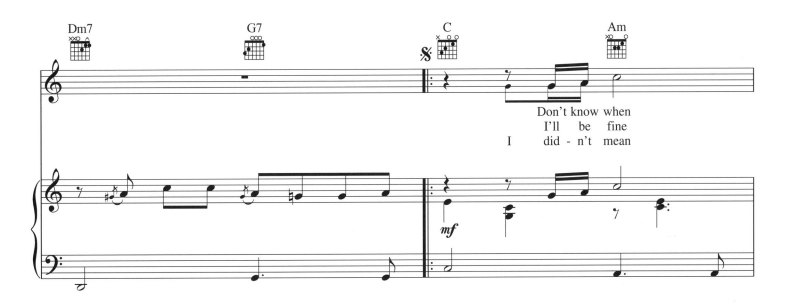

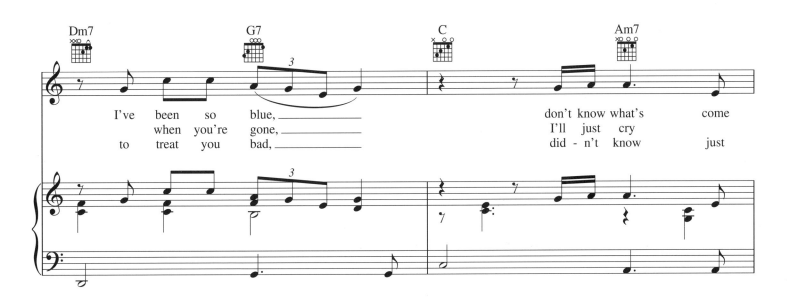

62

EL PASO

Words and Music by
MARTY ROBBINS

Moderato

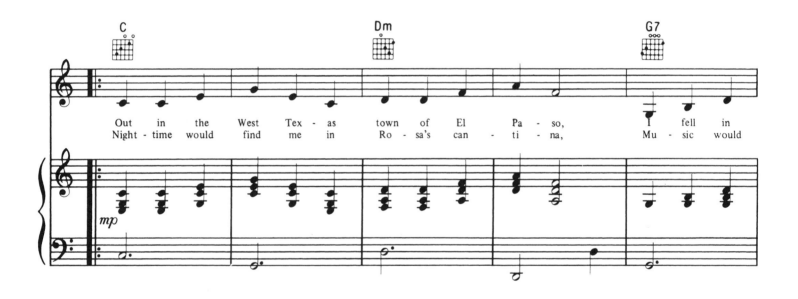

Out in the West Tex - as town of El Pa - so,
Night - time would West find me in Ro - sa's can - ti - na,

I fell in
Mu - sic would

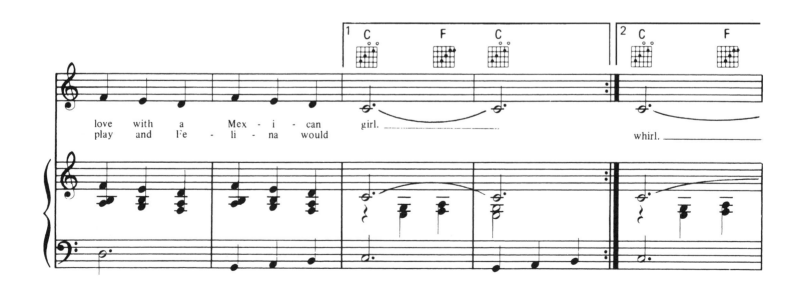

love with a Mex - i - can girl. ____
play and Fe - li - na would

whirl. ____

FOR THE GOOD TIMES

Words and Music by
KRIS KRISTOFFERSON

FEELS SO RIGHT

Words and Music by
RANDY OWEN

FOREVER AND EVER, AMEN

Words and Music by PAUL OVERSTREET
and DON SCHLITZ

GENTLE ON MY MIND

Words and Music by
JOHN HARTFORD

Additional Lyrics

2. It's not clinging to the rocks and ivy planted on their columns now that binds me,
   Or something that somebody said because they thought we fit together walkin'.
   It's just knowing that the world will not be cursing or forgiving when I walk along
   Some railroad track and find
   That you're moving on the backroads by the rivers of my memory, and for hours
   You're just gentle on my mind.

3. Though the wheat fields and the clotheslines and junkyards and the highways
   Come between us,
   And some other woman crying to her mother 'cause she turned and I was gone.
   I still run in silence, tears of joy might stain my face and summer sun might
   Burn me 'til I'm blind,
   But not to where I cannot see you walkin' on the backroads by the rivers flowing
   Gentle on my mind.

4. I dip my cup of soup back from the gurglin' cracklin' caldron in some train yard,
   My beard a roughening coal pile and a dirty hat pulled low across my face.
   Through cupped hands 'round a tin can I pretend I hold you to my breast and find
   That you're waving from the backroads by the rivers of my memory, ever smilin',
   Ever gentle on my mind.

GOLDEN RING

Words and Music by BOBBY BRADDOCK
and RAFE VanHOY

HAVE I TOLD YOU LATELY THAT I LOVE YOU

Words and Music by
SCOTT WISEMAN

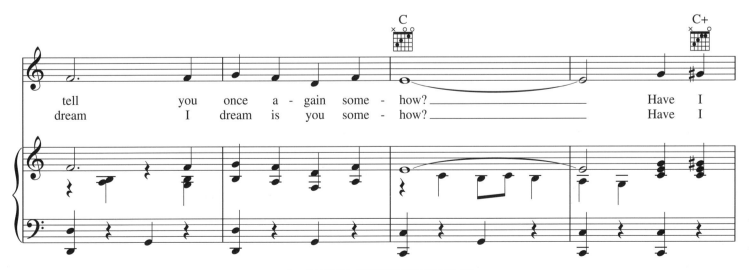

A GOOD HEARTED WOMAN

Words and Music by WILLIE NELSON
and WAYLON JENNINGS

A long time for - got - ten, are dreams that just
He likes the night life, the bright lights and

fell by the way.
good - tim - in' friends.

And the good life he prom - ised ain't what she's
When the par - ty's all o - ver she'll wel - come

HE STOPPED LOVING HER TODAY

Words and Music by BOBBY BRADDOCK
and CURLY PUTMAN

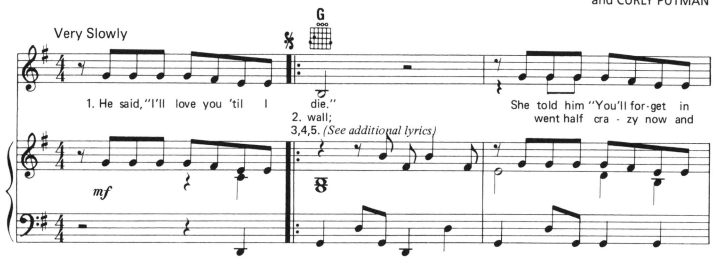

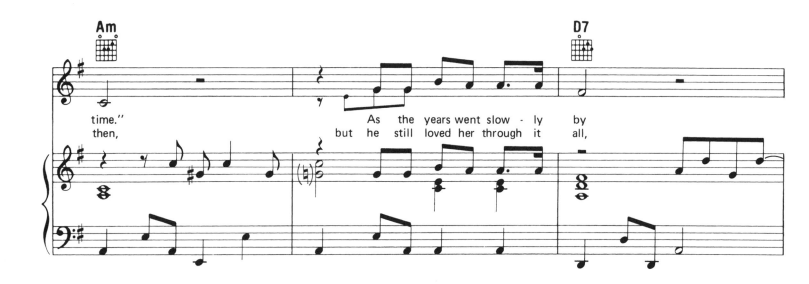

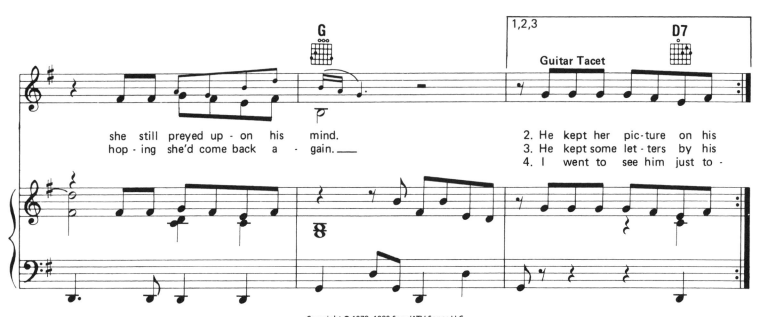

Verse 3:

He kept some letters by his bed, dated 1962.
He had underlined in red every single, "I love you".

Verse 4:

I went to see him just today, oh, but I didn't see no tears;
All dressed up to go away, first time I'd seen him smile in years.
(To Chorus:)

Verse 5: *(Spoken)*

You know, she came to see him one last time.
We all wondered if she would.
And it came running through my mind,
This time he's over her for good. (To Chorus:)

HE'LL HAVE TO GO

Words and Music by JOE ALLISON
and AUDREY ALLISON

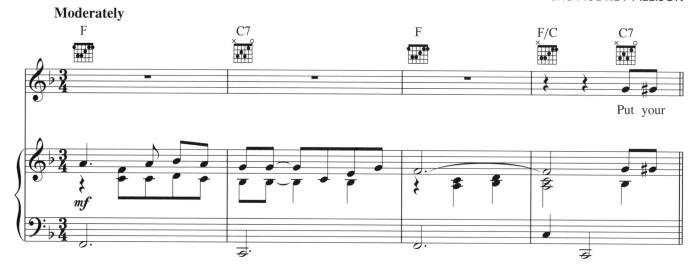

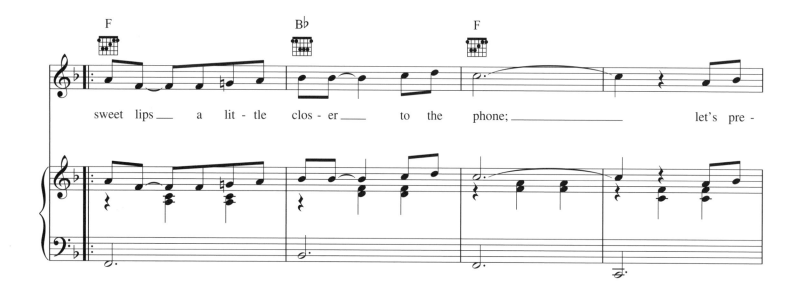

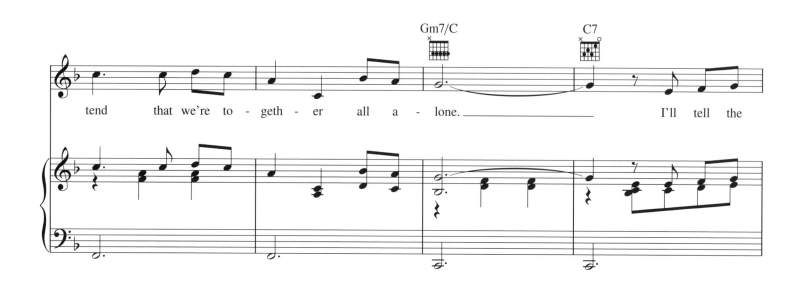

THE HEART WON'T LIE

Words and Music by DONNA TERRY WEISS
and KIM CARNES

* Recorded a half step lower.

HEAVEN'S JUST A SIN AWAY

Words and Music by
JERRY GILLESPIE

HELLO DARLIN'

Words and Music by
CONWAY TWITTY

cry_____ all night 'til dawn.
love_____ so warm and true.

What I'm try - ing to
And if you should ev - er

say find it in your heart to _____ for - give _____ me, _____
is, "I love you ____ and I ____ miss you, ____

I'm so sor - ry ____ that I did you wrong."
come back dar - lin' I'll be wait - ing for ____

Look up

you. _____

HELP ME MAKE IT THROUGH THE NIGHT

Words and Music by
KRIS KRISTOFFERSON

Moderately

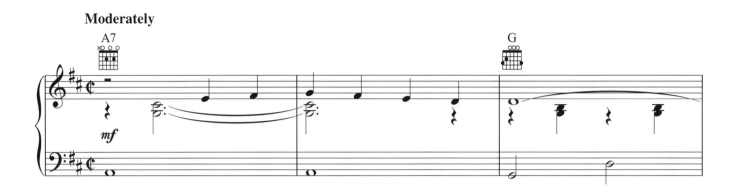

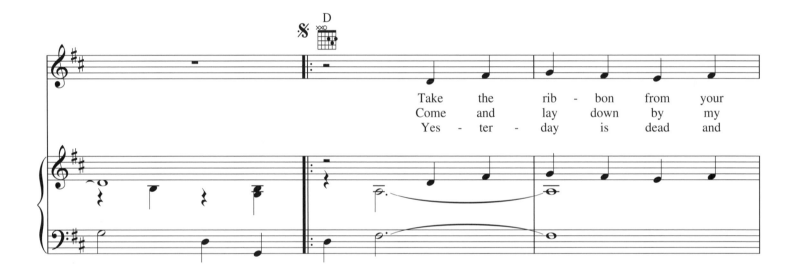

Take the rib-bon from your
Come and lay down by my
Yes - ter - day is dead and

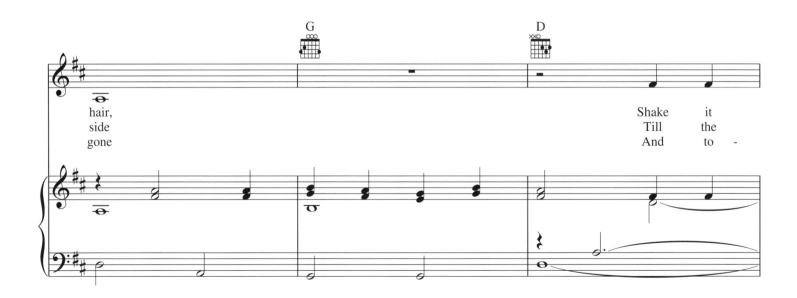

hair,
side
gone

Shake it
Till it the
And to -

loose and let it fall, _____
ear - ly morn - in' light. _____
mor - row's out of sight, _____

Lay - in' soft up - on my skin. _____
All I'm tak - in' is your time. _____
And it's sad to be a - lone. _____

Like the shad - ows on the

wall.

Help me

HOW DO I LIVE

Words and Music by
DIANE WARREN

HOW FOREVER FEELS

Words and Music by WENDALL MOBLEY
and TONY MULLINS

I wan- na know ___ how for - ev - er _____ feels. ___

I BELIEVE IN YOU

Words and Music by ROGER COOK
and SAM HOGIN

Moderately slow, triplet feel

don't be-lieve in su-per-stars,__ or-gan-ic food__ and for-eign cars,__
don't be-lieve that Heav-en waits__ for on-ly those__ who con-gre-gate,__

don't be-lieve the price of gold,__ the cer-tain-ty__ of grow-ing old,__ that
like to think of God as love,__ He's down be-low,__ He's up a-bove,__ that He's

I know with all my cer-tain-ty___ what's go-in' on with you and me___ is a

good thing, it's true; I be-lieve in you.

I don't be-lieve vir-gin-i-ty___ is as com-mon as___ it used to be,___ in

work-in' days and sleep-in' nights,_ that black is black _ and white is white,_ that Su-per-man and Rob-in Hood _ are

I CAN'T HELP IT
(If I'm Still in Love with You)

Words and Music by
HANK WILLIAMS

I CAN'T STOP LOVING YOU

Words and Music by
DON GIBSON

I CROSS MY HEART

from the Warner Bros. film PURE COUNTRY

Words and Music by STEVE DORFF
and ERIC KAZ

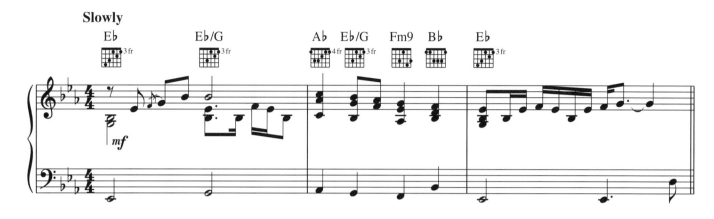

1. Our love is un-con-di-tion-al; we knew it from the start.
2. *(See additional lyrics)*

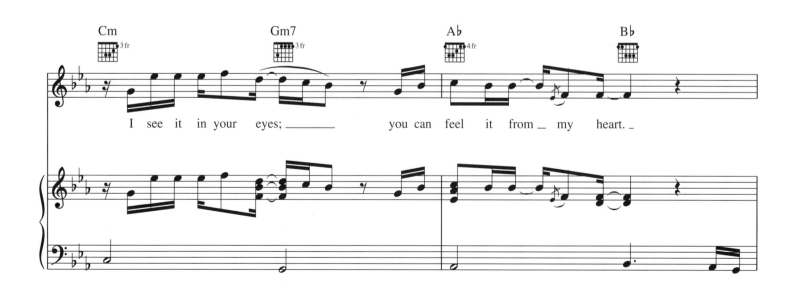

I see it in your eyes;_____ you can feel it from__ my heart.__

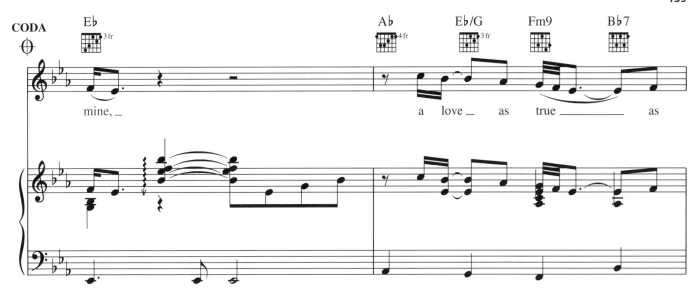

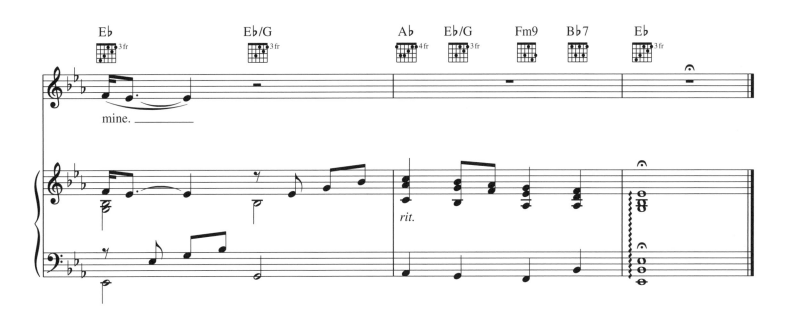

Additional Lyrics

2. You will always be the miracle
   That makes my life complete;
   And as long as there's a breath in me,
   I'll make yours just as sweet.
   As we look into the future,
   It's as far as we can see,
   So let's make each tomorrow
   Be the best that it can be.
   (To Chorus:)

I FALL TO PIECES

Words and Music by HANK COCHRAN
and HARLAN HOWARD

Moderate Country 2

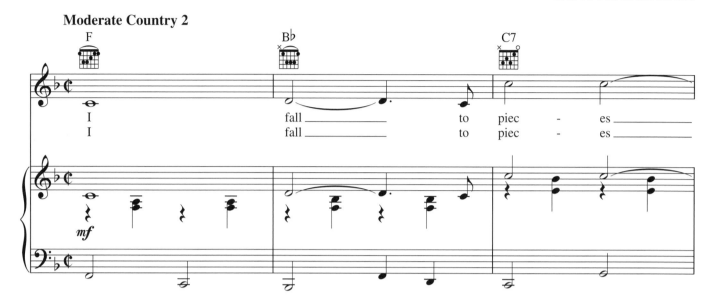

each time I see you a-
each time I some-one speaks your

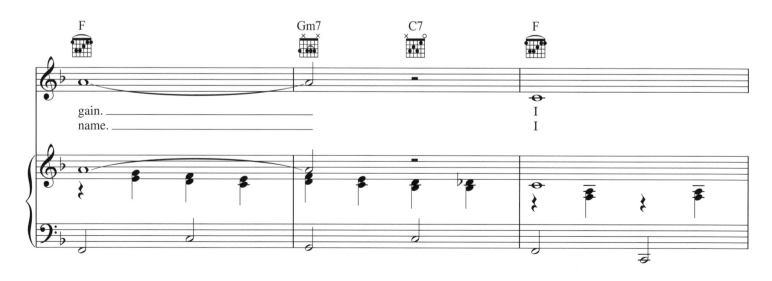

gain.
name.

I FELL IN LOVE

Words and Music by HOWIE EPSTEIN,
PERRY LAMEK, CARLENE CARTER
and BENMONT TENCH

1. Hey, I hit town with-out __ a clue, __ mind-ing my busi-ness like I
2. *(See additional lyrics)*

al - ways do. __ Just __ my luck, I ran smack in-to you. __

And I nev - er could-'ve known it would be like this. You got __

the kind of charm that I can't re-sist. ___ I fig-ure, what's the harm in a

Chorus

lit-tle bit-ty kiss or two? But I fell in love. ___

(What-cha wan-na do that for?) I fell in love. ___

(What-cha wan-na do that for?) I fell in love.

Additional Lyrics

2. I was doing fine out on my own,
Never sitting home by the telephone.
I couldn't complain that I didn't have much to do.
I was a two-fisted woman looking for a fight;
Had a boy on my left, a boy on the right,
But you burn me up like a chicken in a barbecue.
Chorus

I HONESTLY LOVE YOU

Words and Music by PETER ALLEN
and JEFF BARRY

May - be I hang a - round _ here a lit - tle more than I should; we
You don't _ have to an - swer; I see it in your eyes.

both know I got some - where else _ to go. But
May - be it was bet - ter left _ un - said. But

I got some - thin' to tell___ you that I nev - er thought___ I would,   but
this is pure___ and sim - ple   and you must re - a - lize   that it's

I be - lieve___ you real - ly ought___ to know. _____
com - in' from___ my heart and not___ my head. _____

I love you,   I hon-est - ly love___ you.

___ you.

I SWEAR

Words and Music by FRANK MYERS
and GARY BAKER

I LOVE YOU

from the Paramount Motion Picture RUNAWAY BRIDE

Words and Music by TAMMY HYLER,
KEITH FOLLESE and ADRIENNE FOLLESE

I MELT

Words and Music by GARY LEVOX,
WENDELL MOBLEY and NEIL THRASHER

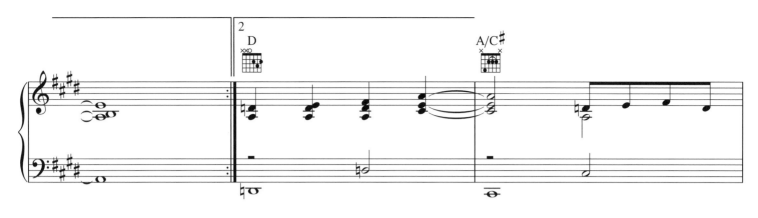

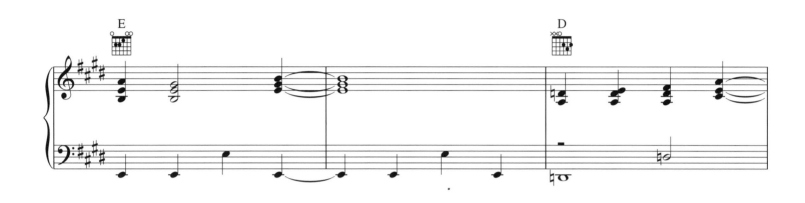

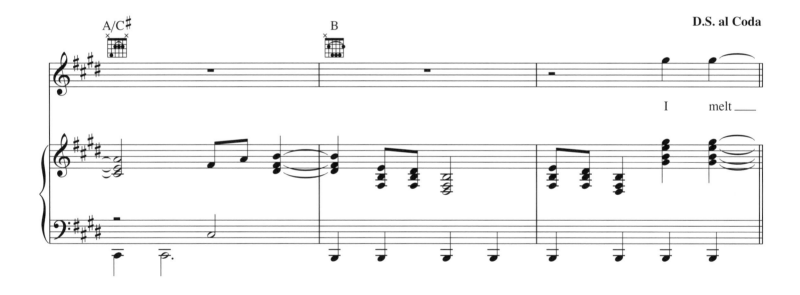

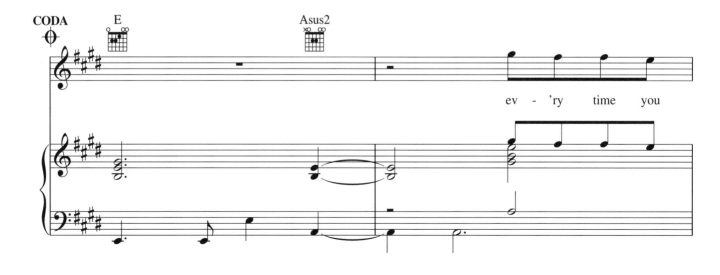

look at me that way. I melt,

I melt.

I STILL BELIEVE IN YOU

Words and Music by VINCE GILL
and JOHN BARLOW JARVIS

Additional Lyrics

2. Somewhere along the way, I guess I just lost track,
   Only thinkin' of myself, never lookin' back.
   For all the times I've hurt you, I apologize,
   I'm sorry it took so long to finally realize.

   Give me the chance to prove
   That nothing's worth losing you.
   Chorus

I WILL ALWAYS LOVE YOU

Words and Music by
DOLLY PARTON

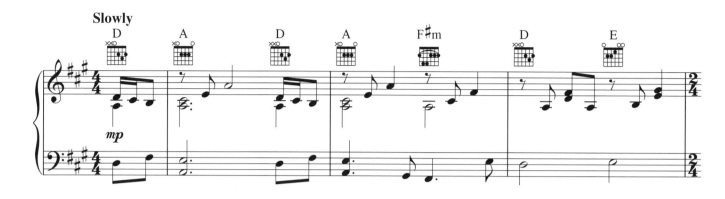

If I should stay,
I would only be in your

sweet mem-o-ries,
that's all I am tak-ing with

*hope life treats you kind
and I hope that you have all that you*

way.
So I'll go,
but I know
I'll think

me.
Good-bye,
please don't cry.
We both

*ever dreamed of.
And I wish you
joy and happiness,
but above*

I WOULDN'T HAVE MISSED IT
FOR THE WORLD

Words and Music by KYE FLEMING,
DENNIS MORGAN and CHARLES QUILLEN

Verse 2.
They say that all good things must end.
Love comes and goes just like the wind.
You've got your dreams to follow,
But if I had the chance tomorrow,
You know I'd do it all again.
(To Chorus)

I'LL STILL BE LOVING YOU

Words and Music by TODD CERNEY, PAM ROSE,
MARYANN KENNEDY and PAT BUNCH

I'M SO LONESOME I COULD CRY

Words and Music by
HANK WILLIAMS

Moderately

Hear _____ that lone - some whip - poor will, He sounds _____ too
ev - er see _____ a rob - in weep When leaves _____ be-

blue _____ to fly. _____ The mid - night train is
gan _____ to die. _____ That means he's lost the

whin - ing low. I'm So Lone - some I Could
will to live. I'm So 'Lone - some I Could

I'VE GOT A TIGER BY THE TAIL

Words and Music by BUCK OWENS
and HARLAN HOWARD

IT WAS ALMOST LIKE A SONG

Lyric by HAL DAVID
Music by ARCHIE JORDAN

Once in ev-'ry life, someone comes a-
You were in my arms, just where you be-

long, and you came to me.
long, we were so in love.

IF YOU SEE HIM/IF YOU SEE HER

Words and Music by JENNIFER KIMBALL,
TOMMY LEE JAMES and TERRY McBRIDE

IT'S YOUR LOVE

Words and Music by
STEPHONY E. SMITH

Male: Danc-in' in the dark, _____

_____ mid-dle of the night. Tak-in' your heart _____

and hold-in' it tight. _____ E - mo-tion - al touch

JACKSON

Words and Music by BILLY EDD WHEELER
and JERRY LEIBER

Moderately

1.,5. We got mar - ried in a fe - ver,
2. go on, my _____ sweet dad - dy,
3. I breeze in - to that cit - y,
4. laugh at you _____ in Jack - son,

I'll be

hot - ter than a pep - per sprout. _____
go a - head and wreck your health. _____
peo - ple gon - na scrape and bow. _____
danc - in' on a po - ny keg. _____

Then I'll

We been talk - in' 'bout Jack - son
Play your hand _____ like a lov - er man, _____ make a
All them wom - en gon - na beg me,
lead you 'round town _____ like a scold - ed hound _____ with your

Ab/Bb   Eb

ev - er since the fire went out. *(He:)* I'm goin' to
big fool of your - self. Go on to
teach 'em what they don't know how. I'm goin' to
tail tucked be - tween your legs. So, go on down to

Ab

Jack - son, _____ gon - na mess a - round. _____
Jack - son, _____ comb your hair. _____
Jack - son, _____ turn loose my coat. _____
Jack - son, _____ you big talk - in' man. _____

Yeah, I'm goin' to
(He:) Got - ta snow - ball _____
I'm goin' to
I'll be wait - in' in

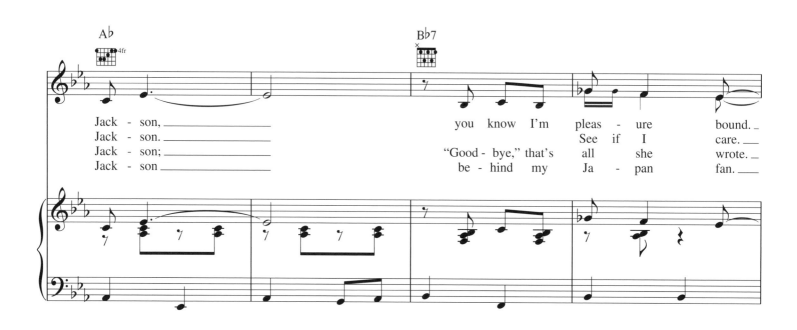

Jack - son, _____
Jack - son. _____
Jack - son; _____
Jack - son _____

you know I'm pleas - ure bound. _
See if I care. _
"Good - bye," that's all she wrote. _
be - hind my Ja - pan fan. _

(She:) Well,
(He:) When
(She:) When they

THE KEEPER OF THE STARS

Words and Music by KAREN STALEY,
DANNY MAYO and DICKEY LEE

KISS AN ANGEL GOOD MORNIN'

Words and Music by
BEN PETERS

Moderately

I've al-ways got a smil-in'____ face,____
The se-cret I'm speak-in'____ of____

an - y - time and an - y____ place,____ And
is a wom - an and a man in ____ love,____ And the

ev - 'ry - time they ask me why, ____ I just smile and say____
an - swer is in this song ____ that I al - ways sing.____

____ You've got to Kiss An An-gel Good-Morn - in' ____ and

MAMA HE'S CRAZY

Words and Music by
KENNY O'DELL

Moderately slow, but flowing

Ma-ma,___ I found some~one,___ like you said would come a-long.
Ma-ma,___ you al-ways said,___ bet-ter look be-fore you leap.

He's a sight,___ so un-like___ an-y man I've known. I
May-be so,___ but here I go___ let my heart lead me. He

was a-fraid to let him in 'cause I'm not the trust-in' kind, but
thinks I hung the moon and stars, I think he's a liv-in' dream, well

LADY

Words and Music by
LIONEL RICHIE

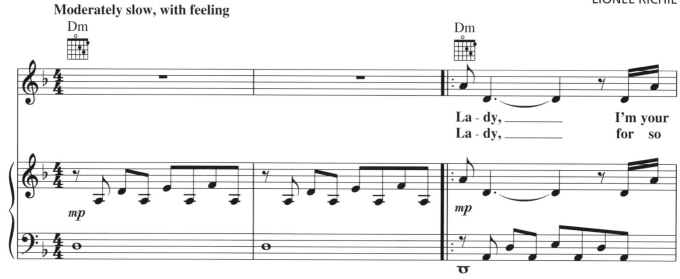

Moderately slow, with feeling

La - dy, _____ I'm your
La - dy, _____ for so

knight in shin-ing ar - mor and I love you, _____ you have made me what I
man - y years I thought I'd nev-er find you, _____ you have come in - to my

am and _____ I am yours. _____
life and _____ made me whole. _____

For -

LOUISIANA WOMAN, MISSISSIPPI MAN

Words and Music by JIM OWEN
and BECKI BLUEFIELD

Recorded a half step lower.

LOVE IN THE FIRST DEGREE

Words and Music by JIM HURT
and TIM DuBOIS

MAKE THE WORLD GO AWAY

Words and Music by
HANK COCHRAN

MAYBE IT WAS MEMPHIS

Words and Music by
MICHAEL ANDERSON

Looking' at you through a mis-ty moon-light, Ka-ty-did sing like a sym-pho-ny.
Read a-bout you in a Faulk-ner no-vel. Met you once in a Wil-liams play.
Ev-'ry night now since I've been back home lie a-wake, drifting in my mem-o-ry.

Porch swing sway-in' like a Ten-nes-see lul-la-by, mel-o-dy blow-ing through the wil-low tree.
Heard a-bout you in a coun-try love song, sum-mer night beau-ty took my breath a-way.
Think a-bout you on my ma-ma's front porch swing talk-ing that way so soft to me.

What was I s'posed to do? Stand-in' there look-in' at you,

ON THE OTHER HAND

Words and Music by DON SCHLITZ
and PAUL OVERSTREET

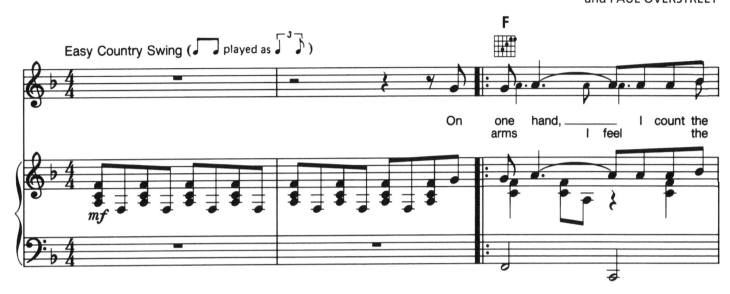

8va bassa

NO ONE ELSE ON EARTH

Words and Music by SAM LORBER,
STEWART HARRIS and JILL COLUCCI

243

ONE MORE DAY
(With You)

Words and Music by STEVEN DALE JONES
and BOBBY TOMERLIN

PAPER ROSES

Words by JANICE TORRE
Music by FRED SPIELMAN

PLEASE REMEMBER ME

Words and Music by RODNEY CROWELL
and WILL JENNINGS

Original key: Db major. This edition has been transposed down one half-step to be more playable.

257

and moon - light falls a - cross your floor

and I can't hurt you an - y - more.

D.S. al Coda

You'll ___ find

CODA

me.

Please _____ re -

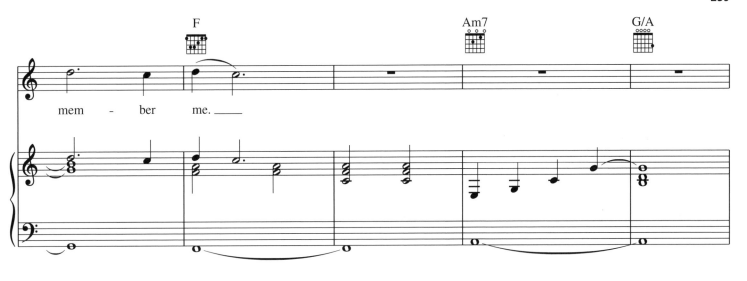

mem - ber me. ____

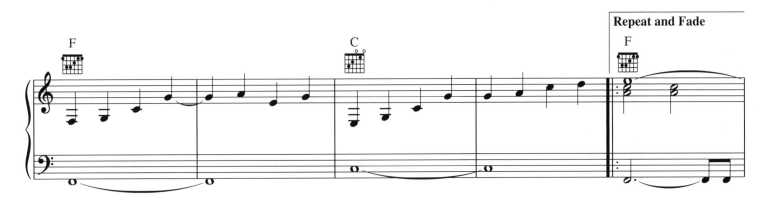

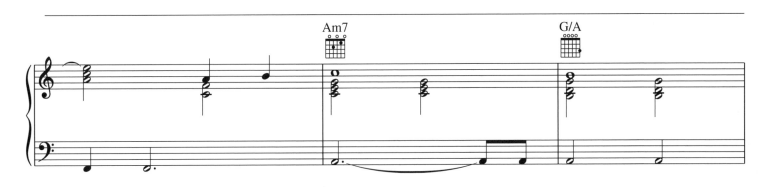

Repeat and Fade

Optional Ending

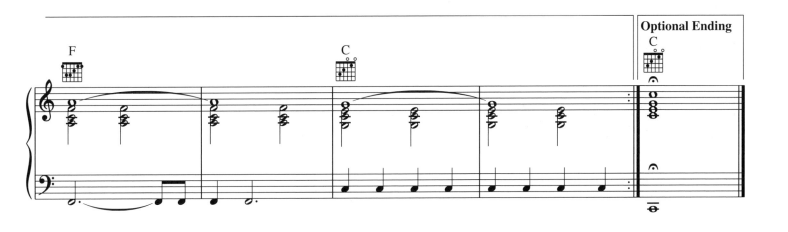

REMEMBER WHEN

Words and Music by
ALAN JACKSON

RING OF FIRE

Words and Music by MERLE KILGORE
and JUNE CARTER

ROLLING IN MY SWEET BABY'S ARMS

(Roll in My Sweet Baby's Arms)

Words and Music by
LESTER FLATT

Very fast Bluegrass

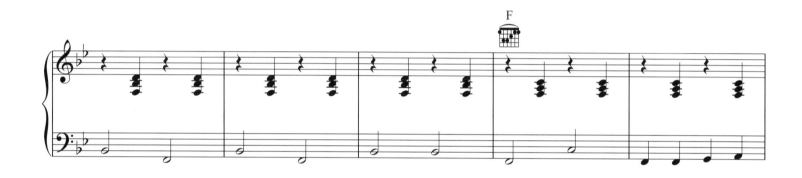

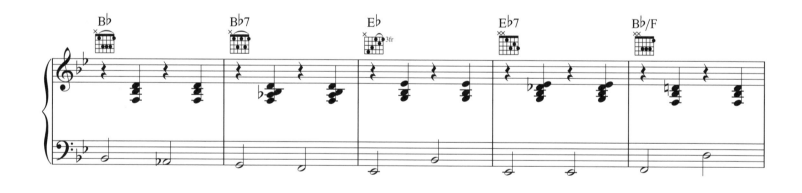

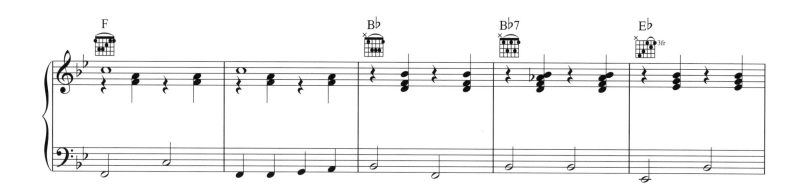

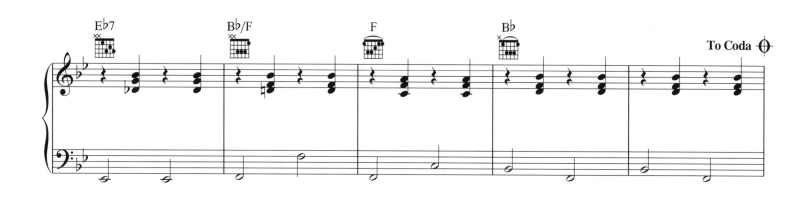

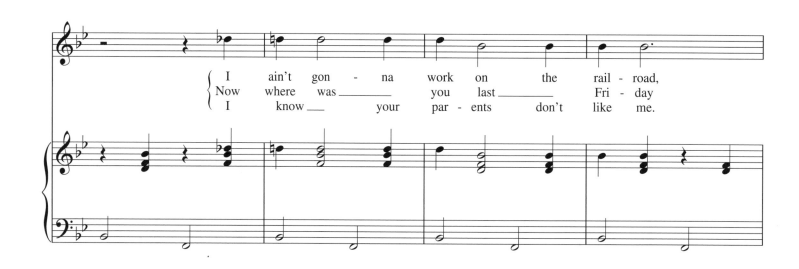

I ain't gon - na work on the rail - road,
Now where was _____ you last _____ Fri - day
I know ____ your par - ents don't like me.

SHE THINKS I STILL CARE

Freely

Words and Music by
DICKEY LEE

SHE BELIEVES IN ME

Words and Music by
STEVE GIBB

SHE'S IN LOVE WITH THE BOY

Words and Music by
JON IMS

*Recorded a half step lower.

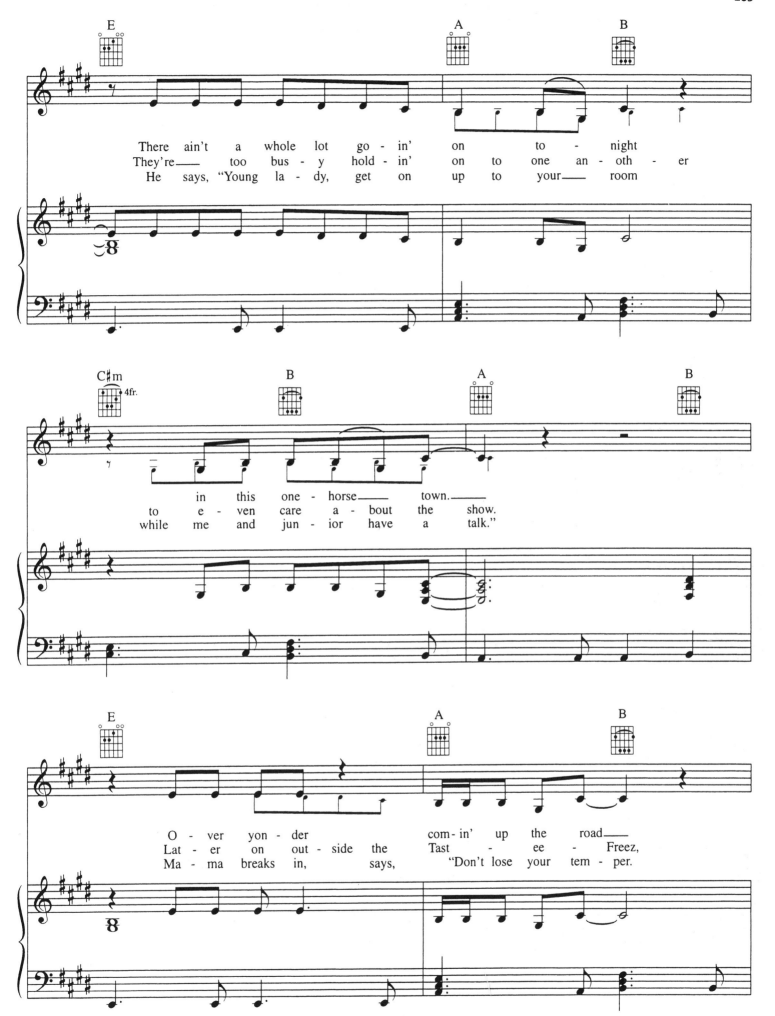

way, she's gon-na mar-ry that— boy some - day.

day.

D.S. al Coda

Coda

D.S. and fade

way. She's in

SHUT UP AND KISS ME

Words and Music by
MARY CHAPIN CARPENTER

Don't mean to get a lit-tle for-ward with you.
Did-n't ex-pect to be in this po-si-tion.
Come clos-er, ba-by, I can't hear you.

Don't mean to get a-head of
Did-n't ex-pect to have to
Just an-oth-er whis-per,

Talk is cheap and ba - by, time's ex - pen - sive. So why___ waste an - oth - er

SOMETHING THAT WE DO

Words and Music by SKIP EWING
and CLINT BLACK

day we be-gin ____ a - gain. ___ Love's not just some - thing that ___

___ we're in, it's some-thing that ___ we do. ___

D.S. al Coda

STAND BY YOUR MAN

Words and Music by TAMMY WYNETTE
and BILLY SHERRILL

STRAWBERRY WINE

Words and Music by MATRACA BERG
and GARY HARRISON

Moderately slow

He was work-ing through col - lege _ on my grand-pa's _ farm. _
I still re - mem - ber _ when thir - ty was _ old, _

I was thirst - ing for knowl - edge
and my big - gest fear was Sep - tem - ber

and he had _ a car. _
when he had _ to go. _

* *Recorded a half step lower.*

© 1996 EMI LONGITUDE MUSIC, ZOMBA ENTERPRISES, INC., GREAT BROAD MUSIC and AUGUST WIND MUSIC
All Rights for ZOMBA ENTERPRISES, INC. Controlled and Administered by EMI LONGITUDE MUSIC
All Rights Reserved   International Copyright Secured   Used by Permission

SWEET DREAMS

Words and Music by
DON GIBSON

SWINGIN'

Words and Music by JOHN DAVID ANDERSON
and LIONEL DELMORE

1. There's _____ a lit-tle girl in our neigh-bor-hood. Her
2.3. (See additional lyrics)

name is Char-lotte John-son, and she's real-ly look-ing good. I had to go and see her, so I

called her on the phone. I walked o-ver to her house,___ and this was go-in' on: 2. Her

Verse 2.
Her brother was on the sofa
Eatin' chocolate pie.
Her mama was in the kitchen
Cuttin' chicken up to fry.
Her daddy was in the backyard
Rollin' up a garden hose.
I was on the porch with Charlotte
Feelin' love down to my toes,
And we was swingin'. *(To Chorus:)*

Verse 3.
Now Charlotte, she's a darlin';
She's the apple of my eye.
When I'm on the swing with her
It makes me almost high.
And Charlotte is my lover.
And she has been since the spring.
I just can't believe it started
On her front porch in the swing. *(To Chorus:)*

THAT'S THE WAY LOVE GOES

Words and Music by LEFTY FRIZELL
and SANGER SHAFER

and that's the way __ love _____ goes."
Guitar solo

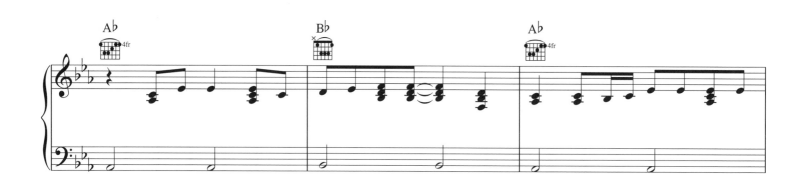

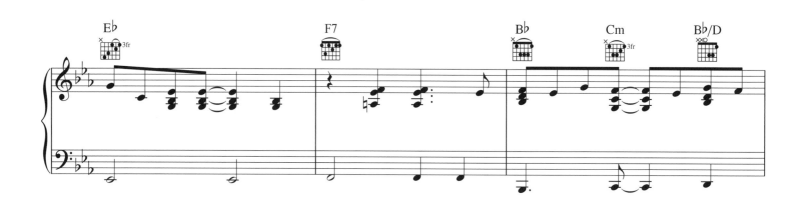

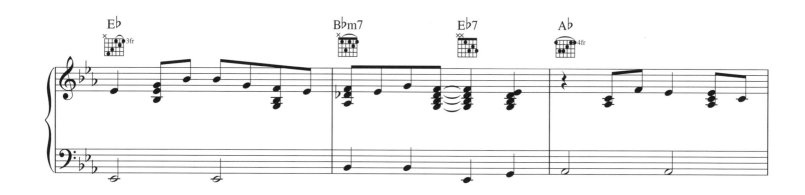

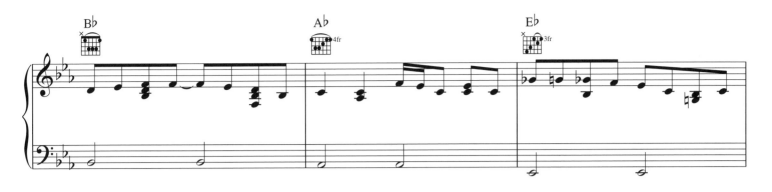

D.S. al Coda

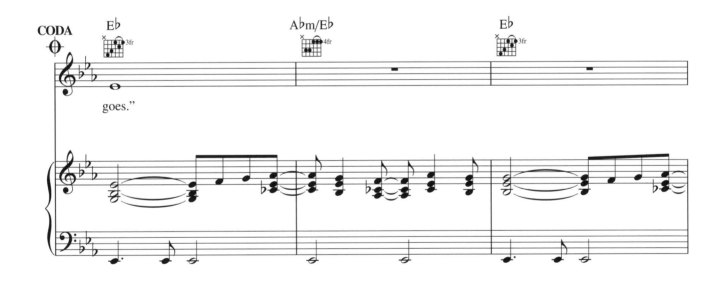

THAT'S WHAT I LIKE ABOUT YOU

Words and Music by JOHN HADLEY,
KEVIN WELCH and WALLY WILSON

Bright Country two-beat

1. I like a man who's cra-zy 'bout me. I like a
2. I like a man who will lay down be-side me. I like a
3. *Instrumental*
4. I like a man who can make it hap-pen, who can get me

THIS KISS

Words and Music by ANNIE ROBOFF,
BETH NIELSEN CHAPMAN and ROBIN LERNER

TIMBER I'M FALLING IN LOVE

Words and Music by
KOSTAS

TODAY I STARTED LOVING YOU AGAIN

Words and Music by MERLE HAGGARD
and BONNIE OWENS

TOGETHER AGAIN

Words and Music by
BUCK OWENS

UNANSWERED PRAYERS

Words and Music by PAT ALGER,
LARRY BASTIAN and GARTH BROOKS

Just the oth-er night ___ at a home-town foot-ball game, ___ my
She was ___ the one ___ I want-ed for all times, ___ and
was-n't quite the an-gel that I re-mem-bered in my dreams, ___ and

wife and I ___ ran in-to my old high ___ school flame. ___ And
each night I'd spend pray-in' that God would make ___ her ___ mine. ___ And
I could tell ___ the time changed me, in her eyes ___ too, it seemed. ___ We

WALKING THE FLOOR OVER YOU

Words and Music by
ERNEST TUBB

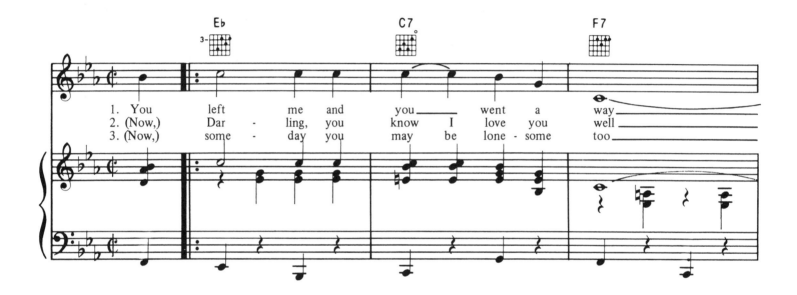

1. You left me and you went a way
2. (Now,) Dar - ling, you know I love you well
3. (Now,) some - day you may be lone - some too

You said that you'd be back in just a day
Love you more than I can ev - er tell
Walk - ing the floor is good for you

WE WERE IN LOVE

Words and Music by ALLEN SHAMBLIN
and CHUCK CANNON

If I could in-vent ___ a time ___ ma-chine, ___
I can still see ___ you when ___ I sleep, ___

then may-be we'd both ___
and there is a pic-

WHAT'S FOREVER FOR

Words and Music by
RAFE VAN HOY

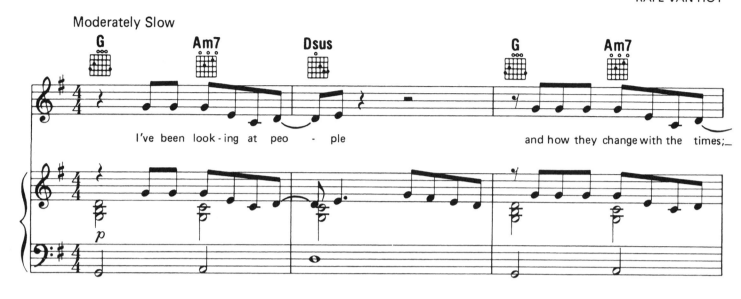

I've been look-ing at peo - ple and how they change with the times;

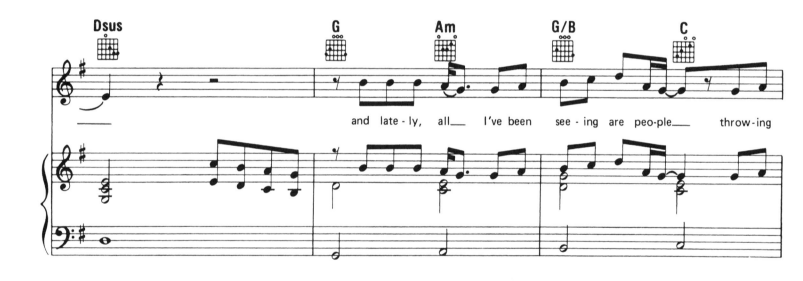

and late-ly, all I've been see-ing are peo-ple throw-ing

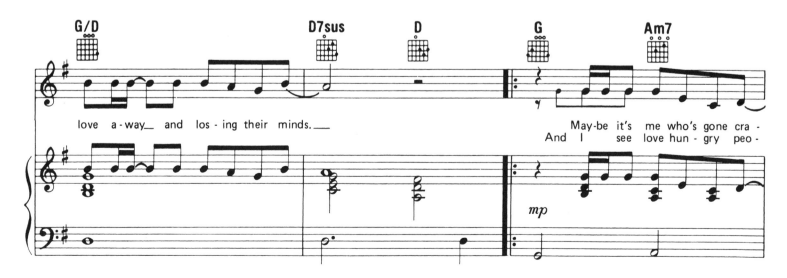

love a-way and los-ing their minds. May-be it's me who's gone cra-
And I see love hun-gry peo-

WHEN I CALL YOUR NAME

Words and Music by VINCE GILL
and TIM DUBOIS

changed, ___ 'cause no - bod - y ___ an - swered when I called ___ your ___
mains. ___ But no - bod - y ___ an - swers when I call ___ your ___

name. ___ The name. ___ Oh, the ___

lone - ly ___ sound ___ of my ___ voice ___ call - ing is

driv - ing ___ me ___ in - sane. And

WHEN I SAID I DO

Words and Music by
CLINT BLACK

1. These times _____ are trou-bled and
2. *(See additional lyrics)*

these times _____ are good, _____ and they're al-ways gon-na be. They

rise and they fall. _____ We take 'em all the way that we

Slowly and freely

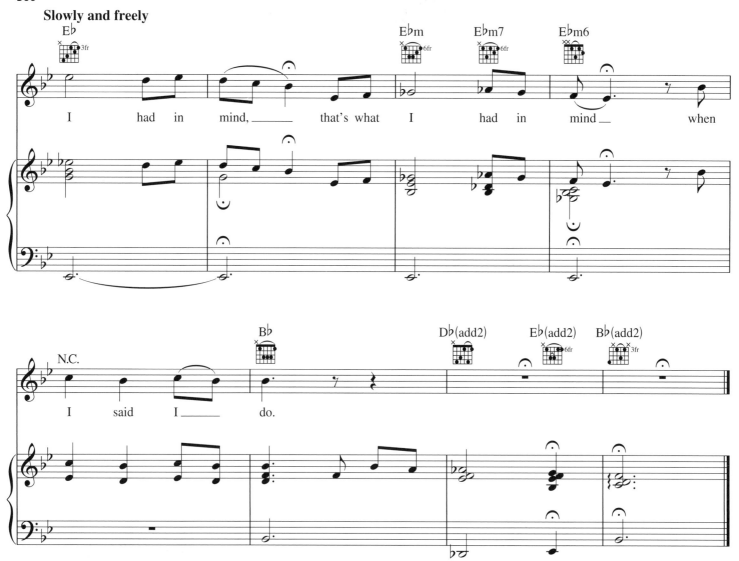

I had in mind, _____ that's what I had in mind _____ when

I said I _____ do.

Additional Lyrics

2. Well, this old world keeps changing,
And the world stays the same
For all who came before.
And it goes hand in hand,
Only you and I can undo
All that we became.
That makes us so much more
Than a woman and a man.
And after everything that comes and goes around
Has only passed us by,
Here alone in our dreams,
I know there's a lonely heart in every lost and found.
But forever you and I will be the ones
Who found out what forever means.
Chorus

WICHITA LINEMAN

Words and Music by
JIMMY WEBB

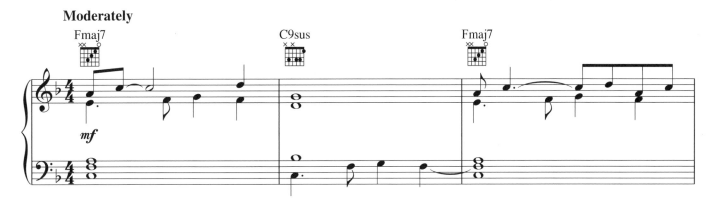

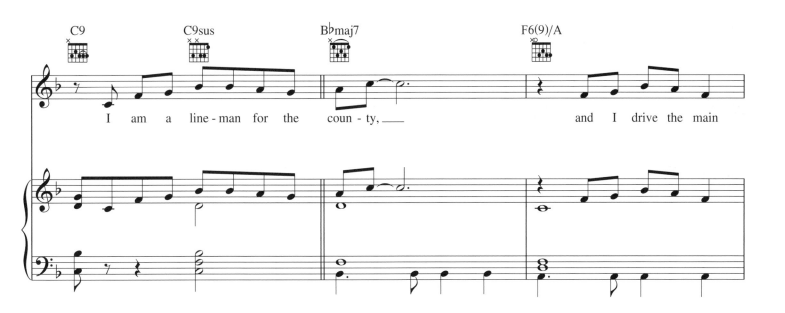

WHEN YOU SAY
NOTHING AT ALL

Words and Music by DON SCHLITZ
and PAUL OVERSTREET

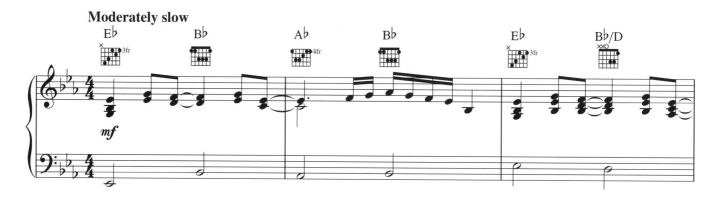

It's a-maz - ing how_ you can speak right_ to my heart._
All day long__ I can hear peo - ple talk - ing out loud,_

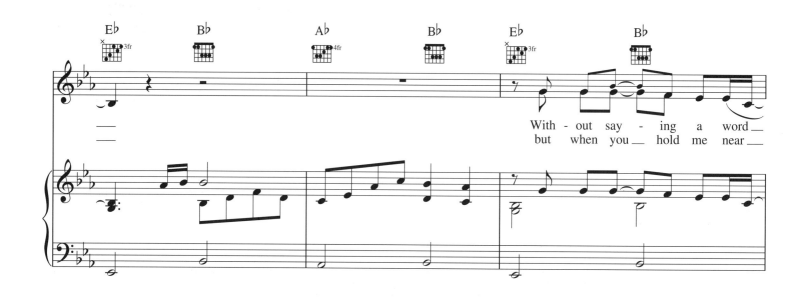

With - out say - ing a word_
but when you_ hold me near_

when you say noth-ing at all. _____

The

when you say noth-ing at all. _____

rit.

WHERE'VE YOU BEEN

Words and Music by DON HENRY
and JON VEZNER

THE WOMAN IN ME
(Needs the Man in You)

Words and Music by SHANIA TWAIN
and R.J. LANGE

Slowly

I'm not al - ways strong, and some - times __ I'm e - ven wrong. But I win when __ I choose, and I can't stand __ to lose. But I can't al - ways

WOULD YOU LAY WITH ME
(In a Field of Stone)

Words and Music by
DAVID ALLAN COE

WRAPPED AROUND

Words and Music by BRAD PAISLEY,
CHRIS DuBOIS and KELLEY LOVELACE

Yes sir, __ I love her ver - y much. I know it's on - ly been sev - en months. __

YOU LOOK SO GOOD IN LOVE

Words and Music by KERRY CHATER,
RORY BOURKE and GLEN BALLARD

YOU'RE STILL THE ONE

Words and Music by SHANIA TWAIN
and R.J. LANGE

YOU'RE THE REASON GOD MADE OKLAHOMA

Words and Music by SANDY PINKARD, LARRY COLLINS,
BOUDLEAUX BRYANT and FELICE BRYANT

Medium Country Blues

There's a full___ moon o - ver Tul - sa I hope that it's shin - nin' on you___ The
nights are get - tin' cold - er in Cher - o - kee coun - try there's a Blue Nor - ther pas - sin' through___
I re - mem - ber green eyes ___ and a ranch - er's daugh - ter but re -

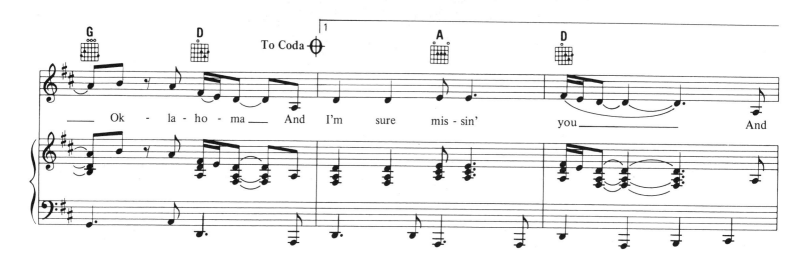

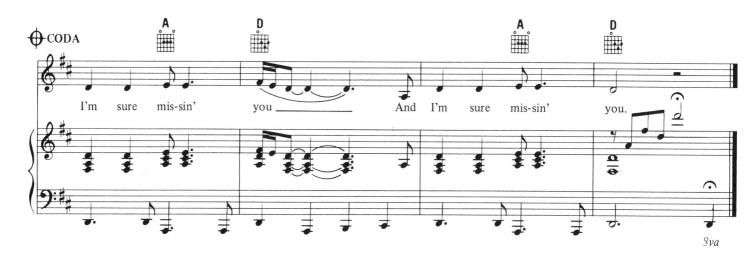

2. Here the city lights outshine the moon
   I was just now thinking of you
   Sometimes when the wind blows you can see the mountains
   And all the way to Malibu
   Everyone's a star here in L.A. County
   You ought to see the things that they do.
   All the cowboys down on the Sunset Strip
   Wish they could be like you.
   The Santa Monica Freeway
   Sometimes makes a country girl blue

   (BRIDGE)

3. I worked ten hours on a John Deere tractor,
   Just thinkin of you all day....
   I've got a calico cat and a two
   room flat, on a
   street in West L.A.

YOUR EVERYTHING
(I Want to Be Your Everything)

Words and Music by ROBERT JOSEPH REGAN
and CHRIS LINDSEY

YOU'VE NEVER BEEN THIS FAR BEFORE

Words and Music by
CONWAY TWITTY

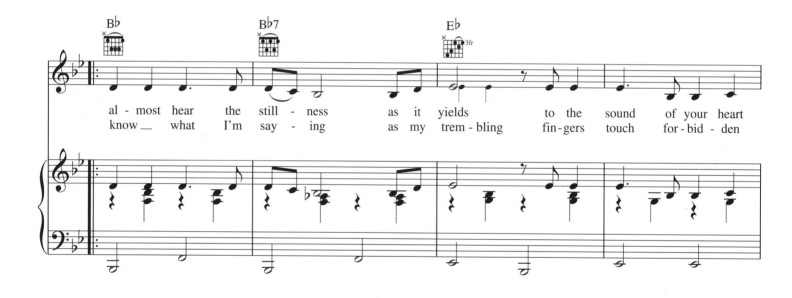